Dear Carol Burnett

A Collection of
Children's Poems
Sent to Carol Burnett

Edited by Sylvia Cross

NASH PUBLISHING, LOS ANGELES

Illustrated by
David Jarvis

Library of Congress Catalog Card Number: 71-167519
Standard Book Number: 8402-1211-9

Published simultaneously in the United States and Canada
by Nash Publishing Corporation, 9255 Sunset Boulevard,
Los Angeles, California 90069.

Printed in the United States of America

First printing

This is a book about love.
Love for your fellow man,
Love for your country,
Love for animals, colors, weather—
Love for God.

Most of it was written by young children.
It's funny—they know where it's at
When most of us adults don't.

They are our future.

When they grow up, will they
Still feel the way they do today?

Do you think, maybe, we could
Raise them that way?

Carol Burnett
Los Angeles, California, 1971

See the World through Children's Eyes

If only we could see the world through children's eyes
we'd see a wonderful thing in a butterfly flying by,

the great fun of flying a kite,
running in fields of golden wheat,
playing in the rain in our bare feet,
climbing in a tree when playing hide and seek,
the joy of stepping stones in a small creek,
if only we could see the world through children's eyes.

Patricia K.
Floral Park Memorial High
Floral Park, New York
Age 18

The Earth's Most Delicate Things

Yesterday
if someone had asked me
to name the world's most
delicate things,

I would have answered
spider-webs,
lace
or butterflies . . .
the taste of wood at dawn.

I would have thought of
moss and pansy petals,
new-born deer
and mosquito wings . . .
the smell of honeysuckle.

But today I hugged a little boy
and saw him smile.

Melanie B.
Country Day School
    of the Sacred Heart
Philadelphia, Pennsylvania
Age 10

Richie

Gee,
It's hard to be Three.
Everyone looks at me
but no one really sees me.
It's hard to be Three.

Gee,
It's tough to be Three.
Some people listen to me
but no one really hears me.
It's sure tough to be Three.

Gee,
It hurts to be Three.
The bigger kids won't play with me.
It seems as if I'm *also* there.
I'd like for them to *really* care.
It hurts to be Three.

Gee,
It's hard to be Three.
There's so many "No's" in life for me.
I'm big enough to ride my trike,
but I can't learn to ride a bike—

I'm tall enough to reach the sink,
but I'm not allowed to get my drink.
I'm old enough to watch T.V.
but I get sleepy at a movie—
so they won't take me.

I can talk as good as they.
Why won't they listen to what *I* say?
Mommy looks at me and winks—and says,
Let's hear what Richie thinks—
Then they all just stare and wait . . .
to hear what I would like to state . . . and I forget.

I can't help it 'cause I'm Three,
and what I say doesn't seem to be
what they want to hear.
They should take the time to see
that all I need to be is *me.*

When I get big and get real tall,
and Daddy wants to talk and all . . .
I'll just pat him on the head, (and say)
Isn't it time you were in bed?

Then he'll be sorry he didn't see
how tough it was, when I was Three.

Joan L.
Los Altos, California
(A mother)

Feeling Low

Why can you not calm my fears
Or dry my burning tears?
Why can you not comfort me
Or reassure me?

Why do you disregard my sorrow
And my thought that *can't* wait for tomorrow?
Why do you act useless when I show you my grief
And only listen for a time that is brief?

I know why it is,
     for you are unable to understand me.
It's the reason you say, "That's not you,"
     for you don't know me.
It's the reason you can't feel my feelings
     or think my thoughts,
But I may be overly harsh, for I know not *yours*
     as you know not mine.

Karin K.
Archbishop Jordan School
Sherwood Park, Alberta, Canada
Age 13

A Mother Is

A mother is someone who loves you from the beginning
    and loves you and loves you until it's the ending.
A mother is someone who cleans up the Friday night mess.
She picks up coke cans and banana peels that aren't a
    bit fresh. A mother is someone who doesn't mind the
    snore, the smell in the bathroom, or the slam of the door.
A mother is someone all powdered and pretty.
A mother is someone warm, wise, and witty.

Lela W.
Lamesa Middle School
Lamesa, Texas
Age 10

Your Little Son

When he is hurt
    you'll shed a tear,
But when he is happy
    your eyes are clear.
When he is sad
    you'll be sad too.
And you'll want him to know
    through and through
That you love him
    very much
And you want him to have
    God's golden touch.

Janice I.
Andersonville School
Laurel, Indiana
Age 10

It Takes a
Certain Kind of Person

It takes a certain kind of person to feel.
It takes a certain kind of person to be real.
A person who is strong.
A person who knows when he's wrong.

It takes a certain kind of person to understand.
It takes a certain kind of person to lend a helping hand.
A person who knows his mind.
A person who knows about mankind.

It takes a certain kind of person to love.
It takes a certain kind of person to be above.
A person who is true.
A person who could be you.

Connie W.
Fort Morgan High
Fort Morgan, Colorado
Age 19

A Thought

Did you ever have a dream?
A dream that you wished, and hoped, and prayed
 would come true?
  Well, I did.

And did you ever take that dream
And place it in your heart
And make a solemn vow to help it along so it
 would come true?
  Well, I did.

And did you ever take that vow
And recite it every night
And do some work to move that dream along so it
 would come true?
  Well, I did.

And did you ever take that work
And put a smile into it
And keep that smile in it to make sure the dream
 would come true?
  Well, I did.

And did you ever take that dream,
That vow, that work, that smile,

And place them in your life, and were sure your happiness
    would be true?
      Well, I did.

And did you ever take that life
And live it to its fullest
And know that you were truly happy?
      Well, I did.
        I am.

Vicky S.
Morton West High
Berwyn, Illinois
Age 18

What About That Good Fresh Air

As a human being
I've been blessed, indeed,
With all the necessities of life
That I'll ever need.
Tall green grass,
Sky, blue and fair,
But, what about that "good fresh air"?

As a human being
I want to be strong.
Fight for what is right,
Defeat what is wrong.
Gasoline fumes,
And oil . . . everywhere,
So, what about that "good fresh air"?

As a human being,
I'll do my best
To fight pollution
With all the rest.
I'll fight to win,
Either cheat or play fair,
But, I'll fight and I'll get that "good fresh air"!

Yes, as a human being
I want to be seen
Bringing up my children

Breathing air fresh and clean.
Running and jumping,
Clean clothes and clean hair,
So let's do something about that "good fresh air"!

Debbie I.
Oscar Rose Junior College
Midwest City, Oklahoma
Age 20

I've Almost Forgot

I've almost forgot what clean is.
When I look at our filthy bay,
Why do we let it continue?
That's where my thoughts are today.

I've almost forgot what beauty is,
What beauty is, or was;
Even my sky isn't blue with fluffy clouds
Just grey, or yellow, with clouds of dingy fuzz.

I almost, even, forget what love is,
When horror surrounds me on the streets,
White against black, young against old
And goodness everending in defeat.

Yet, this is everyone's world,
Tho hate-filled, dirty and sad.
Can't we get together, and overcome the bad?

Sandra G.
Roosevelt Grade School
Tampa, Florida
Age 11

Walls

I looked in front of me and what did I see
    a wall before me
I looked to the side and what did I see
    a wall beside me
I turned around and what did I see
    another wall behind me
I looked to the side and what did I see
    the last wall beside me
Is this the life I am to lead
What could the matter be with me
If I cry and plead
Will you release me
From these walls of fear, pain, hunger and suffering

Patricia K.
Floral Park Memorial High
Floral Park, New York
Age 18

Care

Care is something that you show,
Care is something that you know.
The thing about care that I like so much
Is care is a feeling, it's impossible to touch.

Care can be shown in the most marvelous way,
Such as simply saying, "How was your day?"
"Be careful when you cross the street."
Say "Hi" to whoever you meet.

There are many ways to express care,
But at many places it's very rare.
There's a lot of people in this world today
That never hear someone say, "I care."

There are many definitions
For the word C-A-R-E.
I pay no attention to them
Whatever they may be.

The definition that I stick to
Is the meaning that I feel is true.
"Care" is just saying
"I love you."

Melodie W.
Apache Junction School
Apache Junction, Arizona
Age 12

Love

What is love? A pile of leaves,
Or rays of the sun?
Does it come in all colors,
Or does it just come in one?

Joseph H.
Stevens Elementary
Bethlehem, Pennsylvania
Age 9

People

People are all the same,
Some may be white, and others black,
But they're still people.
They all live on the same earth,
And they all must in some way
Feed, clothe, and shelter themselves.
An even larger task for all people
Is to learn to live together,
To live with each other and forget the different skin colors,
To realize they are all God's children,
Sent here for a purpose,
And no matter where they live,
Or what the color of their skin is,
They must open their eyes and see,
People are people!

Debbie S.
Pike High School
Indianapolis, Indiana
Age 16

Love

Love is something that can't be helped:
Everyone has it;
No one can live without it.
Love is something everyone does and lives different.
Without Love there is no friendship.
It is bad enough with love;
With war and hate.
Without love no one could live peacefully.
Love is hope and peace with people.
Love will exist until the end of time.
Love is beautiful.
It is something that can't be helped:
Everyone has it.

Linda B.
Fremont Junior High
Apache Junction, Arizona
Age 11

Love

Love is when you have a friend
Who gives you the top of his popcorn
Where all the butter is.

Love is having a daddy
Who says he'll let you marry him
When you get old enough.

Love is when you get a rock from your girlfriend
And that rock is her good luck charm
That she wouldn't give to ANYONE!

And love is when pretty ladies
Say that they think little kids are nice.

Debbie B.
George O. Barr School
Port Byron, Illinois
Age 8

Love Is Beautiful

Love is dancing and kicking high,
Love is trees beneath the sky.
A sister wished for, and finally gotten,
Is love's way of showing you were not forgotten.
Parents who love their children so,
Is the love I get wherever I go.
Love is beautiful as you see,
When someone I love, also loves me.

Amy D.
P.S. 200
Flushing, New York
Age 9

Happiness

Happiness is having a mother, a father, a sister
  and a brother.
Happiness is when seeds begin to grow
  and flowers begin to show.

Happiness is getting toys and sharing them
  with other little girls and boys.
Happiness is when the war is done, and I hope
  there will never be another one!

Tracy K.
St. Marks Avenue School
Brooklyn, New York
Age 9

Being Alone

Being alone
Can sometimes be
A normal, pleasant thing for me.

A time for thinking,
For searching inside
To find the self I'm trying to hide.

For feelings to come out,
Good and strong,
That have been hiding all along.

To look real hard,
For many a year,
And never get any further than tears.

To also pull back
From many a friend
Just to see around the next bend.

To look into
The future ahead,
And end up crying on my bed.

To stand upon
A beautiful hill,
Alone, quiet, peaceful and still.

Many a time,
I wander by,
Just looking up into the sky.

Wondering what
Will happen as I roam.
Very lonely, lost and alone.

Jami D.
Winfield Junior High
Winfield, Kansas
Age 13

Before You Go

As I come walking through this door,
I see you sitting on the floor.
You have something in your hand.
You say you're going to another land.
But let me tell you something before you go,
Something I think you ought to know
About the friends who showed you the way.
I want you to see where they are today.
First, there's Jean; she's lying in her bed.
But I doubt that she will speak to you.
She's always staring straight ahead.
Then there's Doug; he's tried before.
He says he'll quit—after just one more.
Paul never lets you down, he'll say.
He kept his promise until today.
Now it's a prison term he must pay.
But mostly I want you to think about Ray.
It was suicide, some say.
But we know it didn't happen quite that way.
I wish you could talk to your friends today.
I know they didn't want things this way.
They'd have different things to say.
They'd say: "Think about us before you go."
After all, they've been there.
They know.

Debbie E.
Alwood School
Alpha, Illinois
Age 15

"What Is"

What is a house without a home,
What is a rhyme without a poem?

What is a child without a toy,
What is a girl without a boy?

What is a lamp without a shade,
What is a book without a page?

What is the sky without a star,
What is near without afar?

What is love without another?
Love is being with each other.

What is grass if it's not green,
What is a river without a stream?

What is the moon without the sun,
What is a loss when you've never won?

Without all these things what would there be?
There might not even be a you or a me.

Sandra R.
Glenbard West High
Glen Ellyn, Illinois
Age 15

A Beautiful Land

I like to play,
And I like to ride
On my black horse
Over the countryside.

The hills are pretty
When the grass is green.
The birds are all singing
And the air is so clean.

Then at last I look up,
I have ridden too far:
The sun has gone down
And in the East is a star.

Carol B.
Anselmo-Merna Public School
Merna, Nebraska
Age 8

I Wonder

I often wonder to myself as I kneel down in church;
If God remains upon that cross in the center of
    the church.

I wonder if God ever goes outside and walks along
    the street;
And sees all the different people that make this
    world complete.

I wonder if God, while walking down the street,
Sees the little boy in the ghetto crying because he
    hasn't had enough to eat.

I wonder if God sees the agony on a soldier's face
As he is told that his best buddy was blown up
    and of his body there is
    left no trace.

I wonder if God sees, while walking down the street,
The anger and hatred in the people's faces
Just because of their different nationalities or
    races.

I wonder if God sees, while walking down the street,
The young people high on dope trying to end their
    strife;
But they learn too late that dope does not end their
    strife but only takes their life.

I wonder if God, after seeing all this,
Doesn't think of the past and reminisce

Of days of old, where so simple life used to be;
But now life is difficult and hard and filled with
agony.

I wonder if God returns to his perch
On the cross in the center of the church.

I wonder if God doesn't raise his head to the skys;
And in the quietness of the church,
softly cries.

Colleen K.
Spring High School
Westfield, Texas
Age 16

A Dream

A Dream is a thing that you see with your eyes,
    It has no shape, it has no size.
You can't touch a dream, but you know it's there.
    A Dream can be anywhere.

A Dream could be happy. A Dream could be sad.
    A Dream could be good. A Dream could be bad.
A Dream is a simple thing, from the future, present or past.
    It may go very slowly. It may go very fast.

You can dream any time of the day.
    When you're at home or when you're away,
When you're working, playing or whatever you do,
    Just remember A Dream cannot be taken away from you.

Maria D.
Memorial Junior High
Valley Stream, New York
Age 13

I Had a Dream

I had a dream
And this dream I shall never forget,
For it had my best friend in it.

This dream I had
I shall always remember
Although my best friend is gone forever.

Mary R.
Hagen School
Sterling, Colorado
Age 11

Forgetting

when people live
 they forget,
but when they die
 they regret
the times that they
 forgot

Sue S.
J. I. Case High
Caledonia, Wisconsin
Age 17

Dream World

I had a dream the other night;
It seemed so very real to see.
There was no sorrow, doubt, or fright—
I dreamed you really wanted me.

When I awoke I cried so much,
I thought I'd never smile again.
For I'd left the dreamland's peaceful touch
And come back to the World of Men.

A hating, cruel world, I know,
With little hope. How sad it seems!
I can't take too much more, and so
I run to safety—the World of Dreams.

I love the world dreams take me to,
Where someone always holds my hand.
I try so hard to dream of you,
To find myself in a different land.

My dreams always seem so real,
The people, plot, the time and place.
And I'm dreaming now, for I seem to feel
Gentle hands on my tear-stained face.

Lorri T.
J. I. Case High
Racine, Wisconsin
Age 17

My Friend

I'm writing a song for you,
    my friend!
I'm writing a song for you.
    This song meant something
to me, my friend!
    This song was meant for you!

I'm writing a note for you,
    my friend!
I'm writing a note for you.
    This note meant friendship to me,
my friend(s)!
    This note is friendship for you!

This note, this song, yes, my friend—
Happiness, friendship, and love for you,
    This song, this note, only for you!
Please help me continue to care!

Katherine S.
St. Mary School
West, Texas
Age 12

Beautiful

Everything is beautiful—
people are beautiful, trees, dolls, a T.V.,
flowers, pictures, clothes, dogs, cats, houses,
trophies, the manger.
Even you are,
Carol B.

Lori O.
Valley Winds School
Ferguson, Missouri
Age 8

What is Love?

Love is something you cannot see.
It's with you every day, at any time, and at any place.
Love is all around you. Everybody has love, even if
    they are mean and nasty.
Love could be in the palm of your hands, but the only
    time you can see love, is when it is not only in your
    hands, but in your heart ♥

Alison S.
Old Orchard Junior High
Skokie, Illinois
Age 11

"A Smile"

    Anger is just a snarl away,
yet it can ruin a perfect day.
    Happiness is better,
all the while,
    For it is reflected
by a smile.

    A smile takes but a moment,
and leaves in a flash,
    Yet it expresses an emotion
which is quite unsurpassed.

    It can bring about a feeling,
which is as true as a beating heart.
    It can make a saddened person
one moment's heartbreak short.

    Yes a smile can do many things,
as it brightens someone's day,
    And it is such a pity that it is seen
for only its moment's stay.

John B.
Hancock High
Kirkwood, Missouri
Age 16

The Teacher that Smiled

I once had a teacher that smiled all the time.
She taught me to read and she taught me to rhyme.
She taught me the nouns and she taught me the verbs.
She taught me the meaning of some very long words.

I finished my homework, I did it with care,
Cause I knew the teacher that cared would be there.

But now she is leaving across many miles.
I will always remember the teacher that smiles.

Molly S.
North Junior High
Moorhead, Minesota
7th Grade

"What's Something without Anything"

What's a class without a teacher?
What's a church without a preacher?
What's a pea without the pod?
What's the world without a God?
What's a human without any brains?
What's a window without any panes?
What's a calendar without a number?
What's a mill without any lumber?
What's a street without a car?
What's a beach without any tar?
What's a garden without a flower?
What's a machine without any power?
What's . . .
But wait a minute, there is one thing we could
      do without and that is POLLUTION.
And I hope we can find a SOLUTION.

Kathy B.
Pierpont School
Ventura, California
Age 8

Reverse Frown

Laughter is a remedy for troubles at hand,
Like fingers and feet tickling through California sand.
Though problems arise and tears may appear,
Laughter carries the water through the atmosphere.

Life seems hard and bitter at times,
People look ahead without you in mind.
But in the crowd, a laugh is heard
And the problem at hand's not so absurd.

The day's work may be of unknown deeds,
And others know more of your wants and needs,
But lift your head to those you're meeting,
Nod, smile, and make a laugh your greeting.

You see, laughter really *is* a remedy
For people everywhere like you and me.
A "reverse frown" on a theatre mask
Making laughter a most worthwhile task.

Debbie I.
Oscar Rose Junior College
Midwest City, Oklahoma
Age 20

A Poem

There's water in the ocean,
There's water in the sea.
If you hold a baby
There's water on your knee.

Bobby M.
Watkins Elementary
Kimberley, B.C., Canada
Age 8

Love

Love is a word. Love is finding a lost kitten
    and holding it on a cold day.
Lover is the name of a cat that had kittens, and
    Little Lover is her kitten's name.
Love is just being with you. And love is holding
    and playing with your new puppy called Cleo.
Love is finding out you could have a Halloween party,
    and inviting someone you really like.
Love is getting four new records.
Love is getting a bouquet of flowers on your birthday.
Love is something very very special.

Patricia M.
Bowling Green School
Westbury, New York
Age 12

A Poem

I love the old bedraggled cat,
His fur is silken smooth.
King of all bedraggled cats,
I love him through and through.

Norman B.
Madison School
Phoenix, Arizona
Age 9

good
Four-Letter Words

A four-letter word
    I like to use
        Is love.

Love is for our God.
    Love stands for my family.
        Love is for our country.

A four-letter word
    I like to think
        Is obey.

Obey our God's will . . .
    Obey our God's commandments.
    Obey laws of our land.

A four-letter word
    I like to live
        Is know.

Know how to help.
    Know how to pray.
        Know how to give.

Able, baby, calm, deed,

Ease, free, good, rest;
These words we like best.

Lori M.
and her third-grade classmates
Cleveland Hill Primary School
Cheektowaga, New York

Happiness Is

Happiness is writing
to you when you have
nobody else to write to.
Happiness is to snuggle
up in bed under all
the blankets on a cold night.
Happiness is just being happy.

Patricia M.
Bowling Green School
Westbury, New York
Age 12

Life

Kindergarten; playing house.
Sunday school; a small stuffed mouse.
Little league; your own white kitten.
Your best friend; a lost blue mitten.
Piano lessons; the fort you built.
Tying your shoes; a patchwork quilt.
A baby sister; castles in the sand.
A first step into a wonderful land.

Going steady; is it love?
High school, success you're dreaming of.
Senior proms; and washing cars.
The way you sat and gazed at the stars.
Final exams; your first summer job.
Saturdays when you were a slob.
Learning, hurting; so much strife.
The second step in your growing life.

Marriage; promotion; a stepping stone.
A wife, and children of your own.
The hardships: taxes, unpaid bills.
The special needs that *she* fulfils.
Your soothing words cure your son's scraped knees.

Your talk with him of birds and bees.
Your child's first Christmas; so much joy.
Could you once have been that little boy?

Growing old; "And when I'm gone . . ."
You hope your memory will live on.
The long, long days; you're all alone.
Your grandchildren will soon be grown.
Your life flies by; you stop and think.
It all went by just like a wink.
You try to find a special part
That will stay forever in your heart.

Was it your childhood with its great free fun
That you think might be the very best one?
Or perhaps your youth with such confusion.
Did you ever really reach a conclusion?
Then you think of your maturity,
Of the love and the hope and security.
But you choose old age from all the rest
Because isn't looking back the best?

John H.
University of Toronto
Islington, Ontario, Canada
Age 18

Bears

Bears Bears Bears
On the stairs
Under chairs
Collecting fares
Washing hairs
Millionaires
Everywhere's
Bears Bears Bears

Jeanie N.
Swansea
Denver, Colorado
Age 7

Fun

Fun, Fun, Fun
lying out in the sun
Fun, Fun, Fun
hitting a home run
Fun, Fun, Fun
eating a jelly bun
Fun, Fun, Fun
sleeping after a good day is done

Patricia K.
Floral Park Memorial High
Floral Park, New York
Age 18

My Noisy Alarm Clock

I have a noisy alarm clock,
It ticks so loud and clear.
In the morning my alarm clock
Rings in my right ear.
So every morning all I hear is
Ring ring ring, and when I go down
The stairs my legs are shivering.
And when my mom sees my legs a shivering
She asks me, "Why are you so cold?"
And so I say, "It's just my alarm clock
Is so bold."

Margaret P.
Lincoln School
Oak Park, Illinois
Age 8

The Cuckoo Clock

In our clock is a little bird,
  Every half-hour he is heard.
He isn't even as big as a sparrow,
  And he lives behind a door
  That is very narrow.
He lives in a little brown house,
  And comes out as fast as
  A small, gray mouse.
Below him is a Roman-numeral clock,
  And a pendulum that goes tick-tock.
He may not have very much to say,
  But I enjoy listening to him every day.

Deanna M.
Lincoln Elementary
Atlantic, Iowa
Age 11

Pink

Pink is a pony that runs very fast.
Pink is a color that always will last.
Pink is a castle upon a bright hill.
Pink is a little spot on a bird's bill.
Pink is the panther I see on TV.
Pink could even be letter "Z."
Pink is the blanket on my own bed.
Pink is always alive not dead!
Pink was my sweater a long time ago.
Pink is a famous color you know!
Pink is bologna you wrap in cellophane.
Pink is my very own window pane.
Pink should even take place of the sky!
That's my story of pink, goodbye.

Kelley W.
Rancho Vista Elementary
Rolling Hills Estates, California
Age 9

Halloween Times

Halloween time will be here soon.
The witches will fly to the moon,
And goblins will be out on the streets,
The kids will be out asking for treats.
Pumpkins will be big and bright,
They will also be a Halloween sight.

Sandi C.
Hawthorne School
Mattoon, Illinois
Age 9

Winter

Winter is here and here it shall stay,
For look out the window, there children play.

There, white snow is all around,
Falling on the sparkling ground.

And inside, hot chocolate awaits,
And five cookies on a plate.

Gloria A.
St. John Vianny School
Northlake, Illinois
Age 10

Winter Is

Winter is skating in a pond,
Winter is having heat,
Winter is catching a cold,
Winter is drinking hot chocolate,
Winter is playing in the snow,
Winter is slipping on the ice,
Winter is staying under the covers,
Winter is building a snowman,
Winter is playing games,
Winter is getting buttoned-up,
Winter is seeing snowflakes falling,
Winter is having a wienie roast by the fire,
Winter is fun,
Winter is making up a poem like I just did.

Rosa R.
Our Lady of Guadalupe School
Chicago, Illinois
Age 10

A Poem

As the wind blows
the grass grows.
And as the grass grows
The wind blows.
And as the wind
weeps the grass keeps.

Shelly G.
Riffenburg
Fort Collins, Colorado
Age 7

Flowers

D is for Daisies up on the ground,
P is for Pansies that are quite round.

B is for Blossoms that are so pretty,
And *B* is for my friend named Betty.

L is for Lillies that are so white,
As they float through the water during the night.

Daisy M.
Magnolia Woods School
Baton Rouge, Louisiana
Age 8

The Brook

A light blue brook
　　ripples by.
Broken twigs fall
　　into the brook
　　and float by
　　　　gently.

East and west banks
　　slightly slope up.
Green trees
　　dot the muddy banks.
This peaceful scene
　　changes with the seasons;
But is kept the same
　　in one's mind.

Rebecca H.
Winchester Community High School
Ridgeville, Indiana
Age 16

Don't Let Pollution

Butterflies
Flowers
Caterpillars
Frogs.
Don't let pollution spoil it all.

Layne J.
Glenview Elementary
Fort Worth, Texas
Age 10

Pollution

Pollution is a bunch of trash,
   What will stop it? A lot of cash.
What causes it? The consumer,
   "Oh!" They say, "That's just a rumor."

But it's true, for this very day,
   People are polluting and littering away.
Please let's stop!
   Before the whole world goes "kerplop."

Pollution: The story is sad.
   Pollution: It's very, very bad.

People are polluting the air and water too,
   Gee! There's so much we have to do!

When you see a black smokestack, pouring out smoke,
   You feel so sick, you think you'll choke!

When you see polluted water, all black and slimy,
   Fish can't live there, it's too grimy.

Mankind: It just won't last,
   Unless pollution is stopped . . . *FAST*

Nancy W.
Weaverton Elementary
Henderson, Kentucky
Age 10

Black Dawn

The factories are coughing smoke,
Awful fumes of dirt and grime.
The people of today must realize
We are running out of time.

The rivers and lakes are being filled
With every kind of waste.
Water will soon become a substance
We simply cannot taste.

How long before the skies will darken,
Blotting out the sun?
Bringing blackness everywhere,
Leaving life for none.

How long before the waters turn
From crystal blue to darkest gray?
Without these waters, Death will come
And take all life away.

There may be some who scoff at this,
And many who may yawn;
But pollution will take its toll
And leave us a black dawn.

Hal L.
Robert E. Lee School
Jacksonville, Florida
Age 16

The Sea Speaks

When I came to earth,
    I was fresh and clean.
But now I am old and used.
    My water it turned purple, green.
All the fish that I once
    Fed, float dead upon my wave;
What do they think I am,
    Garbage's grave?

Ducks they float around me,
    Eat my fish and die.
I'm not meant to be poison,
    Is there a reason why!

When my tide has washed,
    Dead fish and garbage on your lawn,
Maybe you'll do more
    Than sigh, nod and yawn.

Mary C.
Edward Town Junior High
Niagara Falls, New York
Age 13

Little World

I am a little world
    They call me Mother Earth;
I am the shoulder of
    Pain, death and birth.

People walk upon my back,
    They fight
They love
    They cry.
They don't pay much attention to me,
    I often wonder why?

Although I am their home,
    Their special place,
They don't take much care of me.
    They litter about my body,
And pollute my seas.

I am like a garbage can,
    On a dirty shelf,
But oh! I won't do a thing
    Because they'll only kill themselves.

Mary C.
Edward Town Junior High
Niagara Falls, New York
Age 13

A Deadly Thing

I will tell you a riddle about a deadly thing
That doesn't hurt or bite or sting.
I get much worse each and every day
And make your skies look dark and grey.
People cause me in many ways,
By factories, cars, and railways.
                    Answer:
Dead you'll be if you don't change your aim,
For POLLUTION is my name.

Wendy G.
St. Lambert Elementary
St. Lambert, Quebec, Canada
Age 11

A Poem

Flowers are orange
Skies are blue,
Tell me
What do you do?

Victoria W.
White Oak School
Santa Susana, California
Age 6

I Wonder

I wonder why,
I wonder what,
I wonder where,
I wonder why people think,
I wonder what people think of me.
I wonder where people think.
I wonder, is thinking a pleasure or sadness or
    is it just a game like jump rope or a dream
    that comes now and then or a dream that comes when
    you think
I wonder?

Kathy R.
West Morgon High
Decatur, Alabama
Age 12

Yesterday, Today, Tomorrow

Yesterday, the town idiot roamed the street.
He asked about life, what it meant and what it needs.
He ate nothing and was weary with a long forgotten
      hunger, not a crumb had he to eat.
At night he slept with a torn coat as a blanket.

Today, the genius roams the street.
Not a care in the world.
He sits in his dining room with venison to eat.
He sleeps in a quilt bed with a feather pillow for
      his head to lay on.

Tomorrow, the philosopher will roam the street,
Preaching good and bad.
He doesn't need a thing to eat, for he lives on the
      words of truth.
When he meets himself (yes the idiot, genius and philosopher
      will meet) he will search in himself for the truth,
      yes he will search in himself for the truth.

Karin K.
Archbishop Jordan School
Sherwood Park, Alberta, Canada
Age 13

An Unpopular Pursuit

Honesty is the greatest of virtues,
Bestowed upon man by himself;
He often complains and blames others,
But it's only the fault of oneself.

To me this is very important;
Not to lie, or cheat, or deceive;
Man is master of hypocrisy,
More so, than I'd like to believe.

Honesty is an endless pathway,
Up a steep, inaccessible hill.
The traps and temptations are many;
Man's usually like "Jack and Jill."

The trek up this hill is forever,
It takes the whole of your life.
Too many men never make it
In the face of misfortune and strife.

I for one wish to climb it,
Up to the highest of heights.
For on top is the kingdom of heaven,
The greatest of all human sights!

Mark H.
Fairplain Junior High
Benton Harbor, Michigan
Age 14

A Tribute to Apollo Eleven

You left our world with many prayers

Not three men, but all earth, conquering this place.
    You've seen what no man ever saw;
    You've touched what no man could.
    You've faced what no man ever faced;
    You've walked where no man would.
The mystery of the moon is gone; we accept the false no longer.
Mars and Venus are surely next, as we become much stronger.
    We thank you for your courage in conquering the new.
    We are blind no longer, but proud, and wise and true.

Vicki D.
Valley High
Albuquerque, New Mexico
Age 15

How About You?

When people make things, they're enchanted and proud of it.

Something you make usually starts with a dream. Then you start working on that dream and try and make the dream come true. When it finally comes true you are proud of yourself and your work and others are too.

Well there's one thing in this world that's not enchanting; It's pollution and I'm not proud of it!

How about you?

Cindy W.
Norland Junior High
Miami, Florida
Age 13

This Is My America

There's a place I go,
every once in a while,
to get things off my mind.
It's quiet, secluded, and out of the way.
It's America, the home of the brave.

I really live here, all the time,
but lately it's been kind of a drag.
I have to go out and buy good water
and carry clean air around in a bag.

To get a look at our once beautiful cities,
you have to peek through the dirty air.
We used to think London was bad,
Now we're bad and they're just fair.

I'm exaggerating a little, I want you to know.
It's really not that rough yet,
But if we don't do something soon,
It's going to be much worse, I bet.

When it gets back to the way it used to be,
and I can brag about my country,

I'll stroll in the meadows, lie in the grass,
look up at the blue sky
and with very little thought be able to say,
"This is my America."

Debra M.
Monroe-Woodbury High
Monroe, New York
Age 16

What's the News Across the Nation?

What's the news across the Nation?
The ever-growing population.
There's one solution for pollution,
Seeping into our lungs deep down,
There's one answer that can be found.

What's the news across the Nation?
Pollution will lead to citation.
Cutting down forest for transportation,
Fighting for better race relation!

What's the news across the Nation?
Man is killing conservation.
We're using up our earth's resources,
We must take some drastic courses.

What's the news across the Nation?
Wars, Riots, Fights, and Inflation.
Very little education.
The never-ending immigration.

What's the news across the Nation?
We've got the information.
Pot, Barbiturates, LSD—
What kind of place will earth really be?

What's the news across the Nation?
Plowed up fields for cultivation,

Dried up rivers for irrigation!
Is this going to be man's reputation?

What's the news across the Nation?
There has been investigation.
Pesticides like D.D.T.—
Is starting to kill you and me.

What's the news across the Nation?
Everybody wants an explanation.
Will there ever be an end to this—
It is now a big crisis!

Richard D.
Ken M.
Danny H.
Tommy M.
6th Graders, Evergreen Avenue School
Woodbury, New Jersey

What's the Solution?

What's the Solution
To all the Pollution
    That comes from factories and cars,
        Some of it comes from bad cigarettes,
    Some of it comes from cigars.

The Pollution's so thick
It just makes you sick.
    You can't even see for a mile.
        There is so much of that smelly stuff
It dirties your teeth when you smile.

Detergents and bleaches
Poison our beaches.
    We're killing the fish in our streams.
        We're smothering our country in garbage and filth,
Soon all we'll have left will be dreams.

Billy H.
McDowell Elementary
Petaluma, California
Age 10

A Kitten Crying

Alone in the dark I thought I heard my kitten crying. It sounded far off at first, then quite near. It was a cry of distress, a cry of fear mixed with struggle, a hopeless sound.

It kept up at a steady pace and I thought, "I must be dreaming, but I'm only half asleep." I was so tired—too tired to get up. The kitten kept crying.

"I must get up," I thought annoyed, "I can't ignore it any longer." This was a real cry of trouble. What kind of person would I be to ignore such a sound?

"Yes, it keeps crying, I must get up and do something . . . I awoke and realized the crying noise was coming from my own

Do something about air pollution . . .

Before it does something to you.

Patti G.
Cassidy School
Camden, New Jerse
Age 10

Snow

Falling, bumping,
swirling, sparkling,
tiny, silver snowflakes
glisten on the ground.

Robbie K.
Army Trail School
Addison, Illinois
Age 11

Snow

The snow is falling.
Softly, silently,
Blanketing the grey-brown world.
In the country,
It falls in soft, white heaps.
But in the city—
It is churned to slush
Beneath car and truck wheels,
Blackened by factory smoke;
And out on the lake,
It freezes with dead fish.
I wish snow
Could cover the sins of the city.

Philippa C.
Halvergal College
Toronto, Ontario, Canada
Age 14

Let's Find a Solution for Pollution

The cities, factories and cars
Are all the cause of pollution.
It's spreading from here to the stars.
So let's find a Solution for Pollution.

It's killing our insects and bugs.
It clings to our hills and mountains
And close to our cities it hugs.
Also it isn't helping the fountains.

Pollution, pollution please go away—
You're just too much to bear.
And please don't come back to play,
But help us keep America fair.

Jane G.
Central School
Fairbury, Nebraska
Age 11

A Poem (about Pollution)

The sky is blue.
But this isn't true.
It is brown!
Not so much in the town,
Mostly in the city—
This is a pity,
Because it was so pretty.

Debra P.
J. Frank Dobie School
Dallas, Texas
Age 11

Part of Progress

Why should we let the cities
threat our lives in every way?
"It's part of progress,"
People say.
But me, I liked the olden way
back then the sky was very
clear and workers probably still
could hear.
I don't think it's very fair for
people to dirty our air.

The factories nowadays are many.
What costs a dime used to cost a penny.
And then there's litter—what a mess!
I litter too, I must confess.

"America the Beautiful," as the song
goes, what will happen to America?

Nobody Knows!

Jamie F.
Army Trail School
Addison, Illinois
Age 11

South Dakota and I

Happiness is a place in South Dakota.
Opportunity here reaches the quota,
I'm glad I live out here where
There's good clean people and lots of fresh air.

I'm glad for the freedom of the great outdoors,
But only a few miles from the needed stores
There are lakes and parks and camping too.
So many things for me to do.

There are so many places for me to see,
I'm quite positive that you'll agree:
There's the Capitol, Corn Palace, Mt. Rushmore, too
Museums, The Bad Lands and Crazy Horse which is new.

Spring is the happiest time of the year,
Everything comes to life around here:
The grass turns green and the trees leaf out,
Newborn animals run about.

In summer we can play in the sun,
To hike or swim or just have fun,
There are fishing spots and hunting spots in our state
To hike or vacation here is just great.

Autumn is such a beautiful sight,
The trees are dotted with colors so bright,

School bells ring here in the Midwest,
While people and animals prepare for winter's rest.

In winter when the cold winds blow,
We have fun sledding in the silvery snow.
I like to see the pheasants and deer—
My, oh my, I'm never bored around here.

I walk in the pasture with my pet,
to sit on a hill and watch the beautiful sunset.
The fluffy clouds in the blue sky
Make a beautiful background for the birds that fly.

It's fun to sit by the cool blue stream,
Put in my pole and start to dream.
At night the clear sky is full of stars—
You can see the big Dipper—even Mars.

It is my duty to help keep our state clean,
So when people see it no litter will be seen.
Sometimes I wonder how I rate
To be lucky enough to live in this State.

Nancy L.
Chamberlain Public School
Chamberlain, South Dakota
Age 10

Freedom

I'm glad as glad as I can be,
That I'm a child in this country.
I know no hunger. I know no fear.
Because, thank God, I live here.
I may read whatever paper I like,
And go anywhere on my bike.
I may go anywhere I want to pray,
And go somewhere different every day.
I can have a club meeting
Whenever I choose,
And discuss any topic I want to use.
All in all I want to say,
God bless and keep you U.S.A.

Stephanie L.
Fallis School
Denver, Colorado
Age 10